Anc

in Perseverance

Anchored
in Perseverance

Joan Cogan

April 2021

FEAR - forget it and run
OR
face it and risk
"Only you know what the
"it" is"!

Dearest Joyce & Bob —
So very thankful for our
Zion connection — My Bob
could always count on
the two of you for
anything! I am slowly
learning that love and
loss must live in the
same place!

Joan

THE CONNECTION

To every parent that:

- ENTRUSTED me with his/her child
- EMPOWERED me to be the teacher his/her child needed
- INSPIRED me with never-ending enthusiasm every day

To every student that:

- ENTERED my classroom positive, energetic, and respectful
- BECAME a team player eager to learn
- UNDERSTOOD boundaries as we grew together

My story is dedicated to you and anyone I may have interacted with in the classroom. Perseverance is a life skill. It always keeps us plugged into a connection. Although we are wired differently we need each other. We continue to learn from crayons. They find a way to live together in the same box. We can too! Rest if you must, but please don't quit!

RECAP

When the publication of *Anchored in Love* hit the press I soon wore the title first time author. Although I referred to it as a simple story written in segments it was anything but simple.

A - Acknowledge and accept yourself. Really? The deaths of my twin brother Jim and Bob, the better half of 27 years, left me lost.

C - Create your ID. Seriously? I have no clue what that even means.

T - Trust in yourself. Honestly? I better put on my big girl pants and grab whatever courage I can find.

My land anchors did not attempt to fix me. Instead the select few chose to travel with me. I do not want you to walk wounded. I want you to open a door or a window, stay close to nature, breathe, and focus on the present. Consider this an appetizer as we begin to think about persevering together.

PREVIEW

Anchored in Perseverance is a story with two imaginary land anchors, Calvin the cardinal and Abe the ape. Both desperately beg you to keep moving forward when it is much easier to quit. You will meet Max, Sid and Liz. Calvin will spend time with the doubters too. Abe is all about ownership and finding balance. He insists that you understand life is NOT a cruise ship. The roughest storms will prove the strength of your anchors. Remember that perseverance is not a character trait. It is a life skill that you learned as a toddler. That cheering section is still there for you, but you may have to look harder to know who they are. Please don't stumble on something behind you! Look ahead, my friend!

WINDOW OF CAUTION

The purpose of a window is to admit light or air and allow someone to look out. Why are the blinds closed? Perhaps all you see is streaks, cracks, smudges, soap left over from Halloween and a daily gift from the birds. Maybe your vision needs a reality check. Let's explore the ability to persevere together and see what happens.

Why caution?

- You can speed up, slow down, but do not quit.
- You can look out or look up, but do not look down at your cell phone.
- You will soon realize persevering is a life skill that you already possess.

Choose to open the blinds!

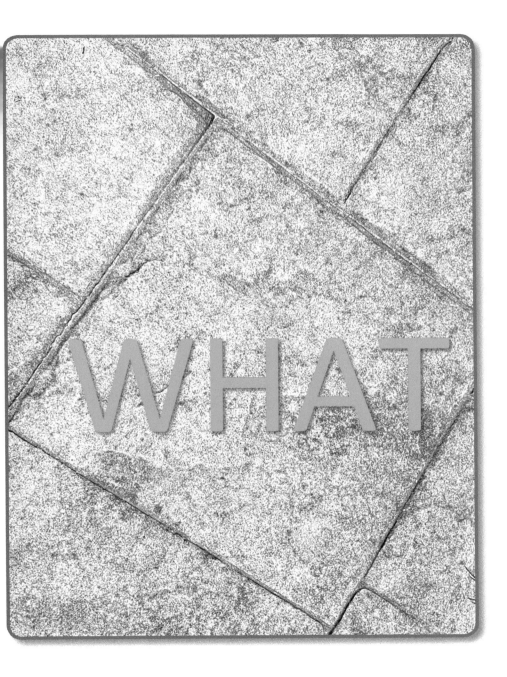

What does it mean to persevere? Persevere is a verb that is calling you to act. It is a doing word. Consider each letter in the word persevere.

P: Plan and Prepare

You have a science project due. What do you need? What will you do if you cannot find a certain item that is necessary to complete it?

E: Embrace and Endure

You find out you are the only boy in your classroom that has been eliminated from wrestling tryouts. Wow - that's dreadfully painful, but you get off the mat anyway.

R: Respond and Recover

You state your intentions. You aim for a spot in the spelling bee. How did you manage to spell celery when the word was salary?

S: Serve and Share

If you are simply out of gas, stuck in neutral or in reverse, can you shift gears? Will you move to the back seat to help others? Often if you do good you begin to feel good. Try it just once and see what happens.

E: Engage and Explore

Take an honest inventory of your feelings when faced with a difficult task. Make a meaningful connection to options you are willing to try. If Plan A does not work there are twenty-five other letters in the alphabet.

V: Visualize and Vocalize

The big hill you are climbing seemingly just turned into a mountain. "I'm too tired. It's too steep. I'm thirsty." This may very well be true, but are you going to turn back or keep going? The choice is yours.

E: Examine and Execute

You are in a rut, maybe even a hole, and you know it. A pattern of behavior has formed that is dull and unproductive. How do you get yourself out before it consumes you? Will you start digging? You decide.

R: Recognize and Receive

Identify one thing that is holding you back. What is frightening you? Gather information. Create a mental image. Is it valid or an inaccurate perception? Take a step or two forward to find out. You must trust yourself.

E: Exhale and Evaluate

Don't overthink yesterday. It is gone. Don't calculate tomorrow. It is not here. Today is a gift, your gift. Breathe, just breathe. Stay in the present.

THINK and DECIDE:

When was the last time you worked hard, really, really hard?

_____

_____

_____

_____

_____

_____

What was your goal? Were you able to reach it?

_____

_____

_____

_____

_____

_____

A FINAL THOUGHT

It takes zero talent to:

- make an honest effort
- be energetic
- maintain a positive attitude
- do a little extra

It is a choice, your choice!

Meet Calvin the Cardinal

Calvin, a beautiful male cardinal, represents all that is good. With striking bright red feathers and a black face mask he captures the heart of those around him. Some believe that he appears when a loved one dies. Others believe he shows up when he is needed the most. Calvin is wise, social, and at times aggressive. He is territorial and does not tolerate anyone messing with his friends. Calvin understands endurance better than most birds. Quitting is not a word in his vocabulary.

- Calvin flew 125 miles per hour, the fastest speed ever recorded.
- Calvin accumulates about 500 air miles per day.
- Calvin is a doer ready for an exciting adventure.

What does an exciting day look like to you?

_____

_____

_____

_____

_____

_____

It was a beautiful fall day when Calvin decided a solo flight to Ohio was in order. He landed in the small town of Canal Fulton. Once he spotted Stinson Elementary School on Erie Avenue he knew this building was perfect. Calvin understood perseverance. He hoped for an opportunity to convince the principal, Mrs. M., that allowing him to enter was a great idea. He promised to listen and obey every school rule.

Are you a rule follower? Seldom? Usually? Always? What is one rule that may be challenging?

_____

_____

_____

_____

_____

_____

WHO else are you going to meet?

- Max - the numbers guy
- Sid - the slug
- Liz - the lunchable gal

Calvin discovers three new friends. Connecting and building relationships is what gives Calvin his strength. It is not muscle strength, but mental strength. Perseverance is often a test, a test of grit. Calvin is a problem solver always willing to take a risk.

How willing are you to step out, maybe just a little, take a risk, a chance? How much grit do you have?

_____

_____

_____

_____

_____

_____

Calvin's adventurous day began in the office of Stinson Elementary School. He quickly introduced himself to Mrs. K., the secretary. It appeared she liked him but wondered what he wanted. Calvin finally convinced her that his goal was to spend time in a classroom, not to cause any trouble. She insisted he sign in and wear a visitor's name tag. Mrs. K. eagerly watched as Calvin used his beak to do as she asked. He then attached the tag to his foot. She discovered Calvin's foot had four unwebbed toes, three claws pointing forward, one claw pointing backward. Calvin knew perseverance was just that. You must keep advancing even though occasionally you lose traction. Onward Math 101!

MAX - the numbers guy

Mr. G., the math teacher, welcomed Calvin into his classroom. He spotted an empty seat next to Max. He soon discovered Max was an overachiever that wanted to be left alone. He knew nothing about perseverance. Calvin learned that Max was extremely bright but did not qualify for the upcoming math tournament. He was anxious, arrogant, and angry. He blamed Mr. G., took no responsibility, felt the test was unfair, and saw himself as the victim. Calvin began to explain to Max that being smart is NOT good enough. Max listened as Calvin offered several suggestions.

- extra effort + willingness = reality
- a goal - blame = step forward
- grit x endurance = a positive
- desire ÷ doubt = a challenge

In two weeks three substitutes will be added to the math tournament roster. Mr. G. is confident Max has what it takes to be on that list. Max knows quitting now is not an option. He wants to participate and will do anything necessary to make it happen. That's perseverance and Max finally understands.

SID - the slug:

Calvin eagerly waited for the recess bell to ring. He wanted to connect with someone unwilling to interact with others. Calvin immediately discovered Sid in damp soil surrounded by a pile of twigs and stones. Calvin introduced himself and Sid quickly responded.

"Oh hi, I'm Sid, the do nothing-deadbeat slug."

Calvin replied, "I sure hope that perception will change, Sid."

Calvin realized if Sid was going to learn anything about perseverance he had to begin building a trusting relationship with him. Although Sid seemed unmotivated with no desire to explore, he liked birds, especially cardinals. He followed Calvin to the monkey bars. His classmates knew Sid was NOT just passing by this time, but he actually wanted to participate. They helped him up as Calvin prepared him for what he had to do next. Grab a bar, let go of the one behind you, swing to grab the next one. Sid did NOT want to let go. He was afraid, but realized it was the only way possible to progress. Before long everyone on the playground encircled the monkey bars. They urged Sid to let go, keep going, and eventually he did. Sid proved to them, but more importantly to himself, that he was able to do it. He was going to continue being a doer. He said goodbye to his sluggish past and welcomed the present. Recess was over. The sound of the whistle signaled everyone to line up and head to the cafeteria.

Liz - the lunchable gal:

Calvin packed his usual lunch of sunflower seeds, mixed nuts, and chunks of apple. He eyed a sad- looking girl sitting by herself and decided to eat with her. Liz nibbled on Swiss cheese and saltine crackers. They soon connected. Liz proceeded to explain to Calvin that she is exactly like the food she is eating, full of holes. The holes of doubt and uncertainty seemed to be consuming her. Calvin abruptly stopped Liz. Negative talk is unacceptable. In order to move forward Liz had to redirect her thinking. In order to understand perseverance Calvin's first goal was guiding her through self-regulation. Liz had to take control of her thoughts, organize her desires, and monitor her behavior. Patching those holes belonged to her, no one else. Liz perked up as Calvin shared more. Rebounding is the ability to bounce back. Begin sorting through the clutter in your mind. Set one goal. Record what you intend to accomplish. Visualize that you can make it happen. Liz was ready to get to work.

Describe a time you felt like Max, Sid or Liz. What did you do about it?

_____

_____

_____

_____

_____

_____

What an amazing morning! Calvin removed his name tag, thanked Mrs. K. for allowing him to visit, and promised to come again.

When do you need to persevere? The bottom line is twenty-four hours a day, seven days a week, fifty-two weeks a year. Perseverance is not a character trait. It is a life skill. You worked hard, regardless of the odds, long before you knew the meaning of perseverance.

Picture yourself traveling an imaginary timeline:

- holding your own bottle, maybe a sippy cup, to drinking from a glass
- discovering your mouth, enjoying finger food, to eating with a spoon
- crawling, standing, cruising, to walking independently
- wearing diapers, perhaps pull-ups, to potty trained
- dressing yourself, buttoning, snapping, zipping, to tying your own shoes
- picking up a ball, throwing it, then catching it with no help
- maneuvering a tricycle, getting training wheels, to riding a bicycle all by yourself

As you continued traveling from babyhood to early childhood you most likely met challenges with confidence. Through messes, spilled milk, bumps and bruises, you embraced learning. Yes, you understood boundaries, but barely survived being told NO for the first time. Your wants, needs, and actions collided with authority. Maybe this was the start of a crash course in perseverance.

Chances, choices, and consequences constantly echoed in your brain. Remember your internal dialogue, what you repeatedly tell yourself, soon becomes your identity.

- I can't do this!
- I give up!
- This is too difficult!

It may have been true for you then, but QUITTING is no longer an option. You must now find a way to redirect your thinking.

- What am I missing?
- Will a different strategy work?
- Can I take my time and approach this task with renewed effort?

THINK:

What does REST IF YOU MUST BUT STAY IN THE GAME mean?

_____

_____

_____

_____

_____

_____

What does COBWEBS OF DOUBT STICK LIKE VELCRO mean?

_____

_____

_____

_____

_____

_____

24/7

Perseverance is a life skill. It is now, NOT later. Please don't look back. Lean into NOT away from difficulty. Take a deep breath, maybe a couple more. You must find a way to stay in the present. Push to persevere. Remember it is NOT a marathon. Focus on moving forward one step at a time.

Why what? If perseverance is a life skill do you really have a choice? It's time to think about Tug of War. It is a contest between two teams pulling on opposing ends of a rope. One eventually drags the other over a centerline. It was a hard fought struggle for power.

Now it is your turn to play. The only difference is you are both teams, Internal Dialogue red and Internal Dialogue green. The game takes place in your head. It involves actively participating and sticking to the task. Who will prevail?

ID red is anxious, eager, and ready to begin pulling. Before long the excuses cloud your thinking.

- I'm tired.
- My arms hurt.
- I'm losing my grip.
- I'll drop the rope and stop.

ID green is just as enthusiastic to start. Before long he too realizes it isn't as easy as he thought it would be.

- I'm tired but I'll take several deep breaths and try harder to focus on the task.
- I'll readjust my grip.
- I'll change the position of my left foot.
- I'm going to keep pulling.

Who prevailed? I want you to hang onto ID green, the internal dialogue that is willing and able to persevere. The choice belongs to you, no one else.

Describe a time when you were indecisive. Did you choose ID red or ID green? What did you learn?

_____
_____
_____
_____
_____
_____

Reminder:

Perseverance is not about how many times you falter. It is about how many times you keep going. It is a goal-directed task. It is the ability to bounce back because you care. Are you able to rebound and then recover? The choice is yours.

There will always be a doubter, the one who hesitates to believe the importance of persevering. He is apprehensive and questions whether it really is a life skill.

Calvin, the wise cardinal, flies in to meet the doubter. Calvin realizes the danger the doubter is creating for himself. He is choosing to build a wall of indifference. Instead of persevering he is hiding from disappointment, uncertainty, sadness, and fear. Calvin senses risky behavior is on the horizon. He challenges the doubter to listen before the wall gets any higher.

- Say goodbye to your past mistakes and forgive yourself during those moments of mounting setbacks.
- Put your ego aside and step out of your comfort zone.
- Realize life is not a remote control. You must get up and change the channel if you expect a different picture.

After hearing Calvin's message the doubter began to question himself. He finally admitted the wall surrounding him was a defense mechanism. It protected him from his insecurities. The doubter turns to Calvin for help.

- Keep your ID in the green zone no matter what.
- Acknowledge the smallest step forward as progress.
- Do all you can to stay focused even when you are scared to death.

Describe a situation that seemed impossible until you successfully accomplished it?

_____

_____

_____

_____

_____

_____

Will you honestly, right NOW, try to answer the question? Why do you need to persevere?

_____

_____

_____

_____

_____

_____

REMINDER:

A flat tire stays flat unless someone changes it. If you choose NOT to change you are NOT going anywhere either.

On his way home Calvin stopped by Lock 4 Park. He happened to overhear a conversation among several adolescents. He decided to join them. They recognized Calvin immediately from his visit to Stinson that morning. Instantly, he was blasted with questions about perseverance.

- How do I persevere when I don't have any direction?
- How do I focus when I much rather party?
- How do I begin to make better choices?
- How do I accept defeat when I planned and prepared, but once again failed?
- How do I let go of my past and find a goal that is meaningful to me NOW?

As I listened to the adolescents speak three particular words caught my attention. HOW DO I? This group knew how vital it is to take ownership. Their ID, internal dialogue, was certainly green. They NO doubt wanted to move forward.

Describe a time you were ready to keep going but had no clue how.

_____
_____
_____
_____
_____
_____

Calvin once again is anxious to share what he knows to be true.

- Reaching out to trusted others is a sign of strength not weakness.
- Life is not a DIY, do it yourself kit. It is not a craft or project that comes with specific directions.
- Defining a purpose to persevere is necessary. You must **name** it, **feel** it, and let it **move** through you.
- Call it a plan, NOT a dream, NOT a wish. Remember a plan has a goal. If you don't have one begin setting one and preparing for one now, yes NOW!
- Strive for progress not perfection.

Since Calvin knew me quite well he insisted I tell the group how I still manage to persevere one day at a time. But how?

Reflection:

Perseverance is a life skill. I am ever so slowly learning to "wear" a very different life. Death forced me to do just that. I am learning to color with a broken crayon.

Much like the adolescents in the park I too was bombarded with questions about persevering. However, my ID, internal dialogue, was fire engine red with no signs of green.

- How do I discover a path forward when the light switch is off?
- How do I begin to swallow uncertainty when I can barely breathe?
- How do I step away from the drama I am allowing others to create for me?
- How do I accept loss and love living in the same place?
- How do I find purpose let alone balance in total darkness?

I desperately needed a friend or two that understood what I was <u>NOT SAYING</u>. Vicky with a Y never flinched. She picked up a torch, lit it, and walked beside me. Without saying a word I knew she was leading me towards uncharted territory. She offered me vision when I had very little, actually none. Before long Vickie with an IE carrying a lantern joined us. Their presence radiated a glimpse of light, a light signaling hope. Not understanding her motive Vicky with a Y extinguished the torch. She reached into the deep pocket of her quilted jacket. She found a battery-operated flashlight, turned it on, and handed it to me. Soon IE Vickie snuffed out the flame of her lantern. The only means of light now was coming from the green flashlight I held. It pointed towards the need to persevere. The loyalty of the two V's <u>silently</u> sent me a clear message: "I'm here for you" and proved it!

REFLECTION: Calvin and I don't want you to lose hope no matter how dark a situation may seem. Walking emotionally wounded often leads to risky behavior. Alcohol / drug addictions and suicidal thoughts spell danger. Drop the <u>d</u> from danger and you are left with anger. Persevering through anger is not easy, but necessary. Please reach out and find the strength and courage to say "I refuse to quit!"

What does YOU ARE THE ARCHITECT OF YOUR OWN LIFE mean?

_____

_____

_____

_____

_____

_____

STAY IN THE GAME

It is time to meet Calvin's dearest and closest ally, Abe the ape. Abe met Calvin as a frightened young cardinal. He was perched in an oak tree afraid to move. He didn't trust the branch and knew for sure it was going to break. Abe's life consisted of eating, playing, and protecting others. How could he protect Calvin? He wants to keep you out of harm's way too! How? The only answer is the ability to trust and use survival skills. That's it. That's persevering!

What advice are <u>you</u> able to give Calvin, the fearful young cardinal?

_____

_____

_____

_____

_____

_____

Abe knew the only solution rested solely in Calvin. He must learn to trust his wings, NOT the branch of the tree. To outsmart his predators he must be prepared to think fast on his feet to survive.

A - accept yourself as you are.

B - believe in yourself no matter what.

E - envision yourself doing it, whatever IT is, in spite of being scared to death.

Calvin wanted to stay in the game and be able to conquer his fears. He chose to listen to Abe's three ground rules.

1. You cannot pick up your glove, quit, and go home.
2. You continue to go to the plate no matter how many times you strike out.
3. You take the field, attempt to catch the ball, regardless of your past errors.

Calvin was afraid to trust. He created his own mental slump. Abe reminded Calvin that pitfalls of a slump are mere excuses not to act. It's much easier to do nothing.

Name two things you have done to survive a dreadful day or a horrible experience.

_____

_____

_____

_____

_____

_____

Abe's Final Word

The only umpire in this game of life is you. You decide what uniform to wear. You choose how many innings you are willing to play. If you choose to STAY a member of Abe's team you will always win regardless of the score. Abe explains exactly how to succeed.

A - attitude - How do you approach a challenge? What is your outlook? A willing attitude often speaks louder than your batting average or brains.

P - purpose - What is your goal as you sort through the slump? It is not found in a bottle, illegal drugs, or self-harm. Whatever the circumstances, my plea, during those dark moments is to stay in the game. Choose to live!

E - effort - Is trying really enough? When exertion and mental energy work together there is no quitting in sight.

Abe, Calvin's ally, has given him a renewed perception of himself. He now has the ability to fly, spread his wings, and protect himself from the hawk that almost devoured him. Calvin's message to you is persevere, persevere, persevere just like you did as a toddler. That's it!

WINDOW OF HOPE

Blinds, what blinds? The view is totally yours. The ability to persevere is not a character trait. It is a choice. You traveled with Calvin as he shared all he knew about perseverance. You walked with me as I searched for understanding with the two V's by my side and a green flashlight. You heard the final word from Abe. He reminded us that through our weakness we often become strong.

Look out that window again. Look up! Let's toast to life!

- a clearer vision
- trust in others
- ability to reach out
- renewed strength

Stay anchored in perseverance no matter what!

Forever Grateful,

Joan

QUILT

Each patch carefully sewn together represents my love and thanks.

- from typist Katie Pettigrew to photographer Laurie Traganza
- from the quilters of St. Jacob's Lutheran Church to Lashell Williamson for leading the way
- from Outskirts Press who worked towards the publication

Who else?

- from the dream team of nine to their parents, my nieces and nephews
- from the community of Northwest Local Schools to the Schalmo YMCA, especially director Pam Leddon
- from those who continue to embrace me as family minus the blood connection.

Anchored in Perseverance,

Joan

CPSIA information can be obtained
at www.ICGtesting.com
Printed in the USA
JSHW051057280920
8203JS00003B/52